Sea Shell
Coloring Book

Get FREE printable coloring pages and discounted book prices sent straight to your e-mail inbox every week!

Sign up at:
www.adultcoloringworld.net

ISBN-13: 978-1535537681
ISBN-10: 153553768X

PREVIEWS:

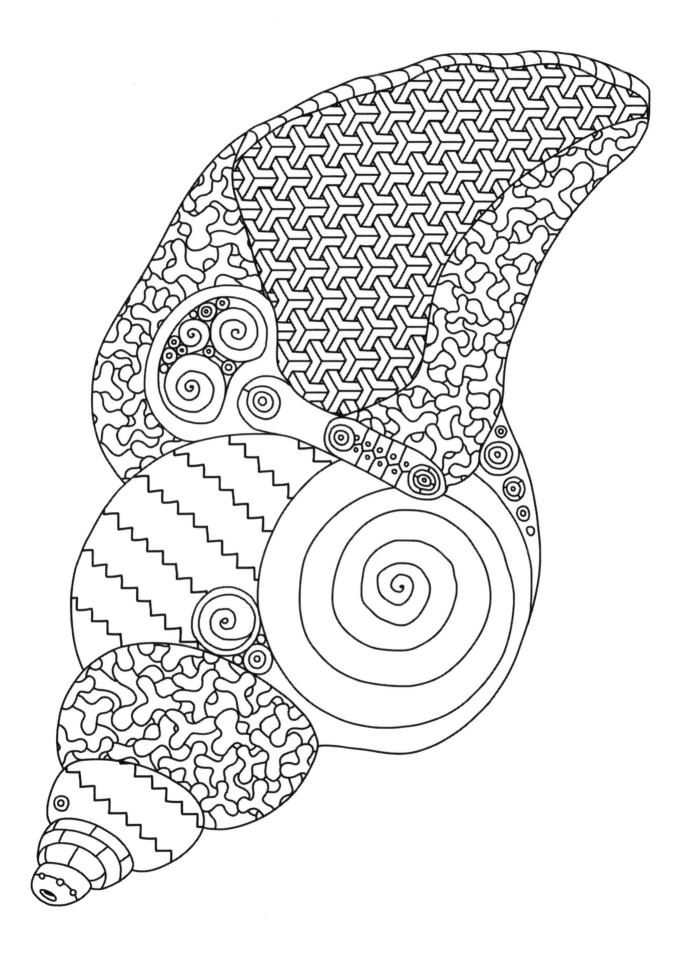

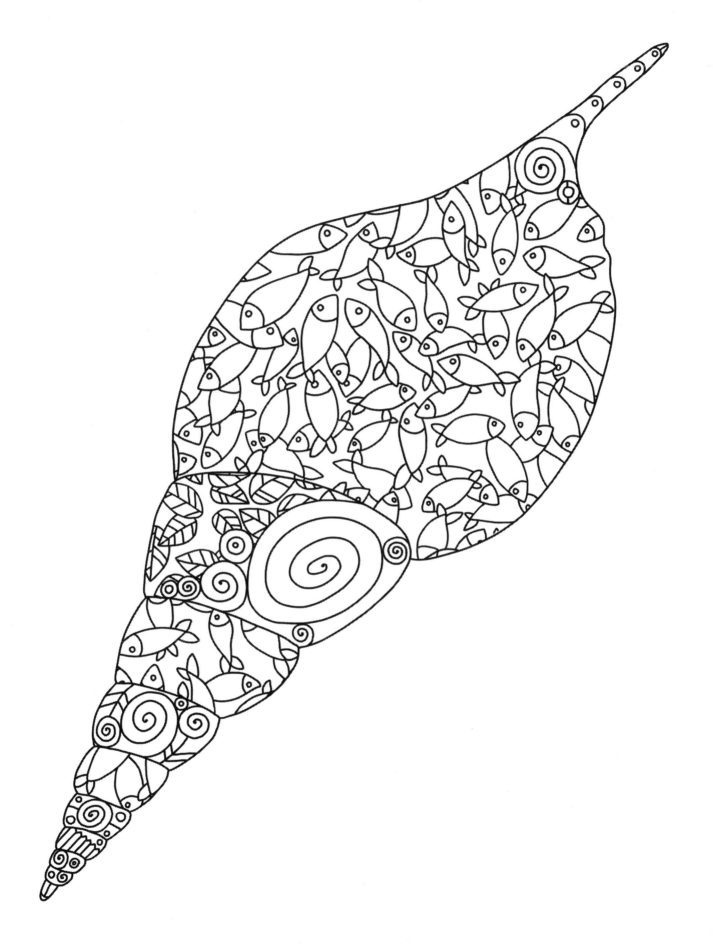

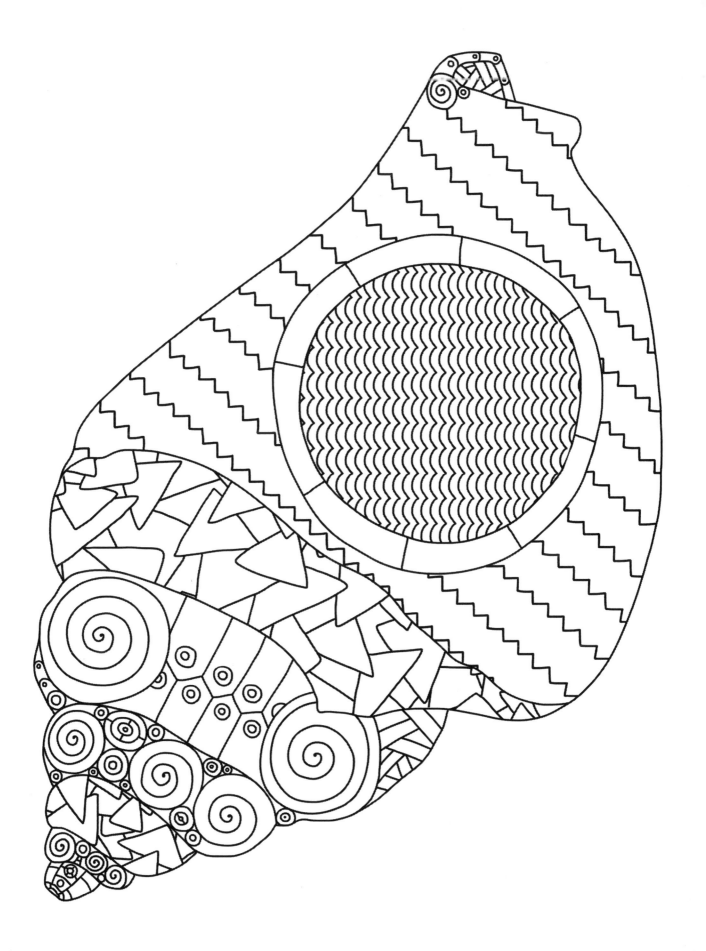

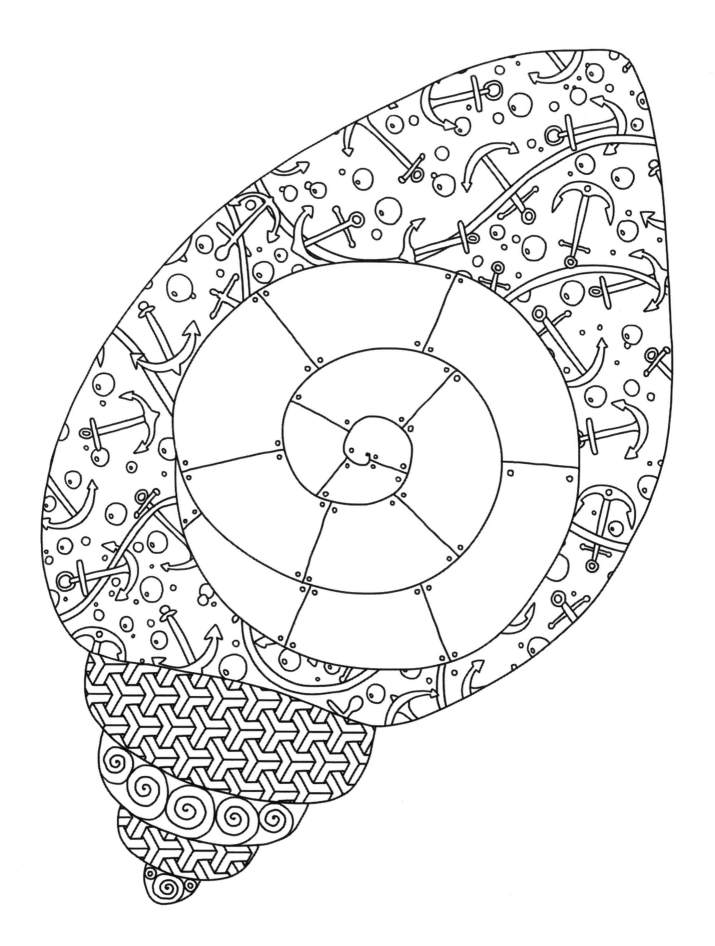

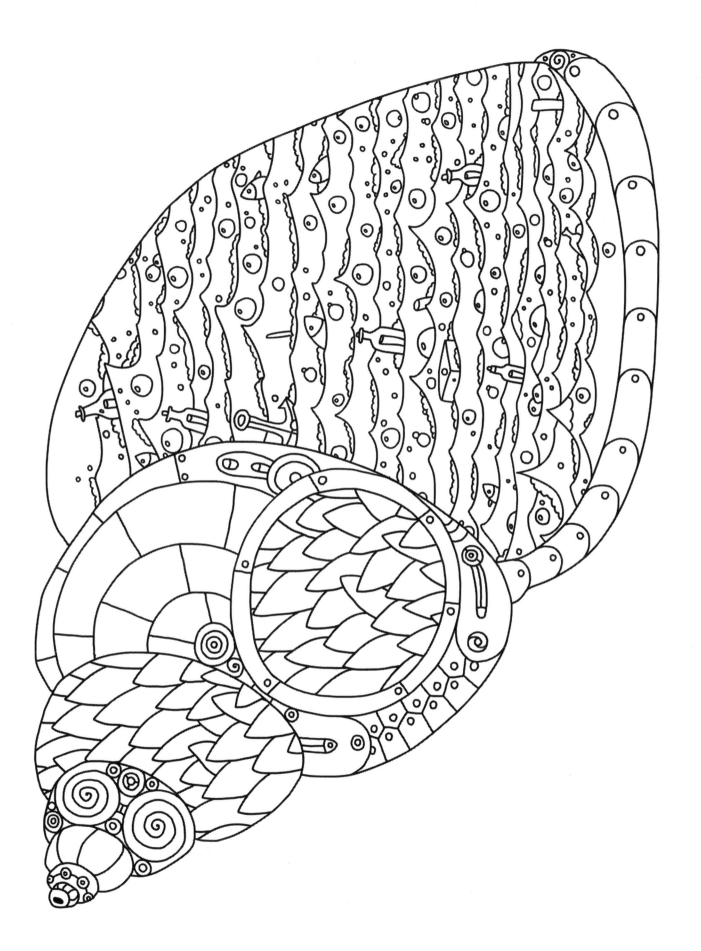

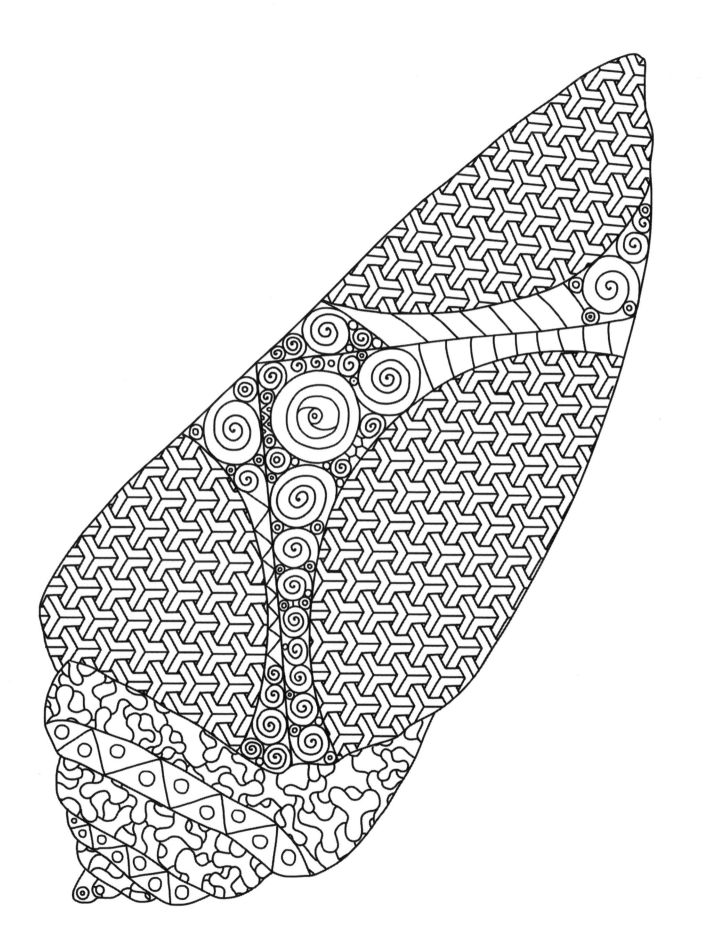

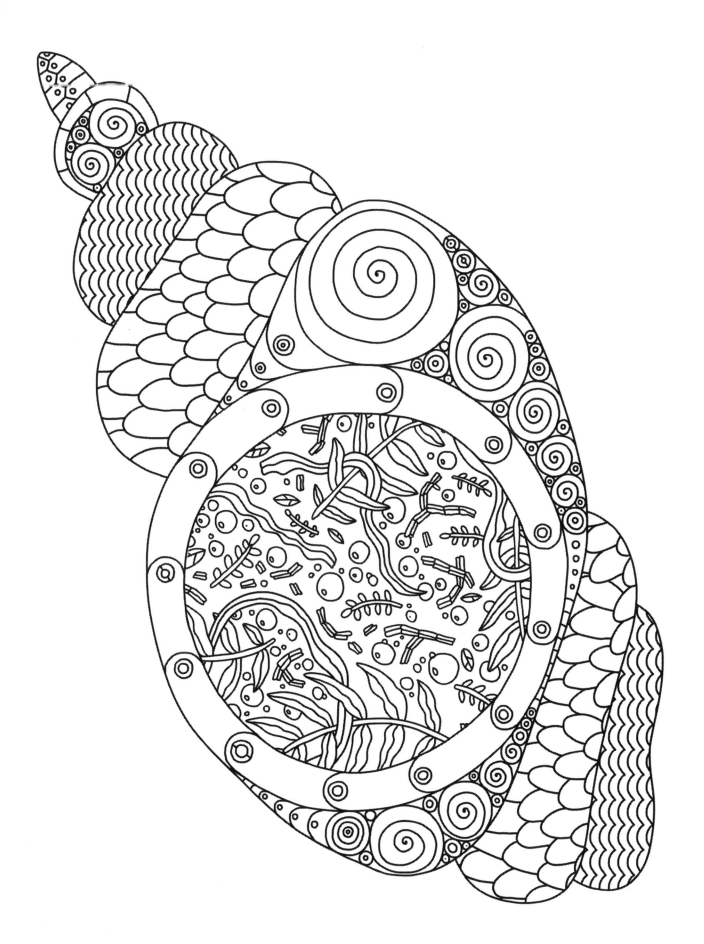

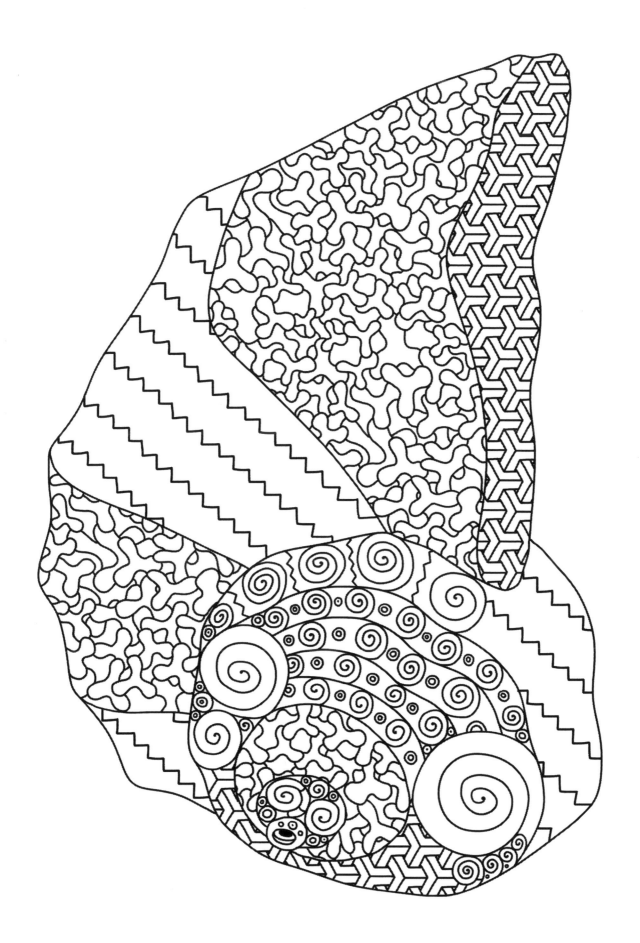

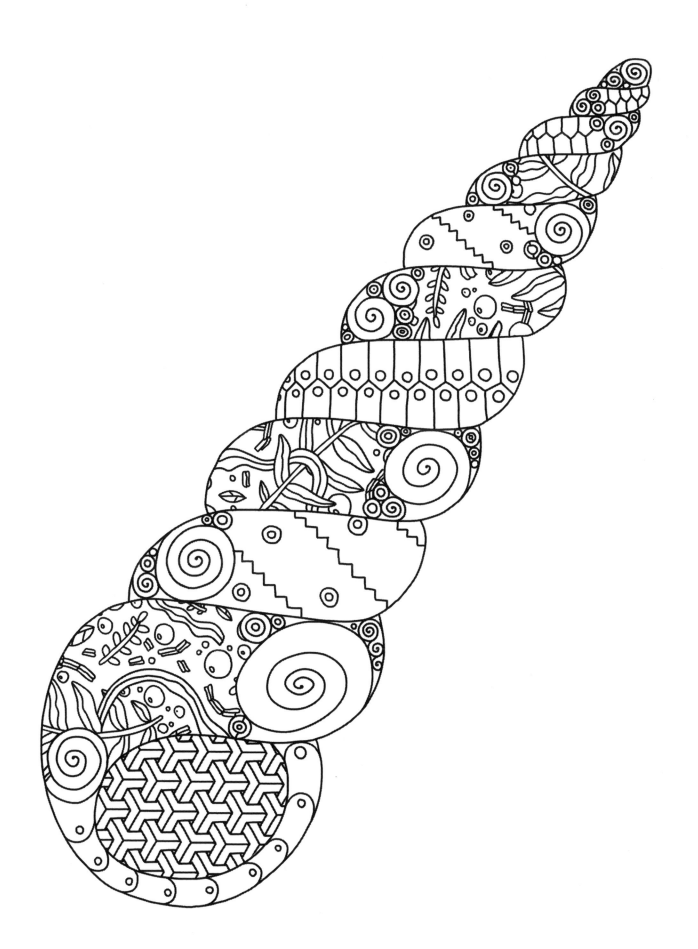

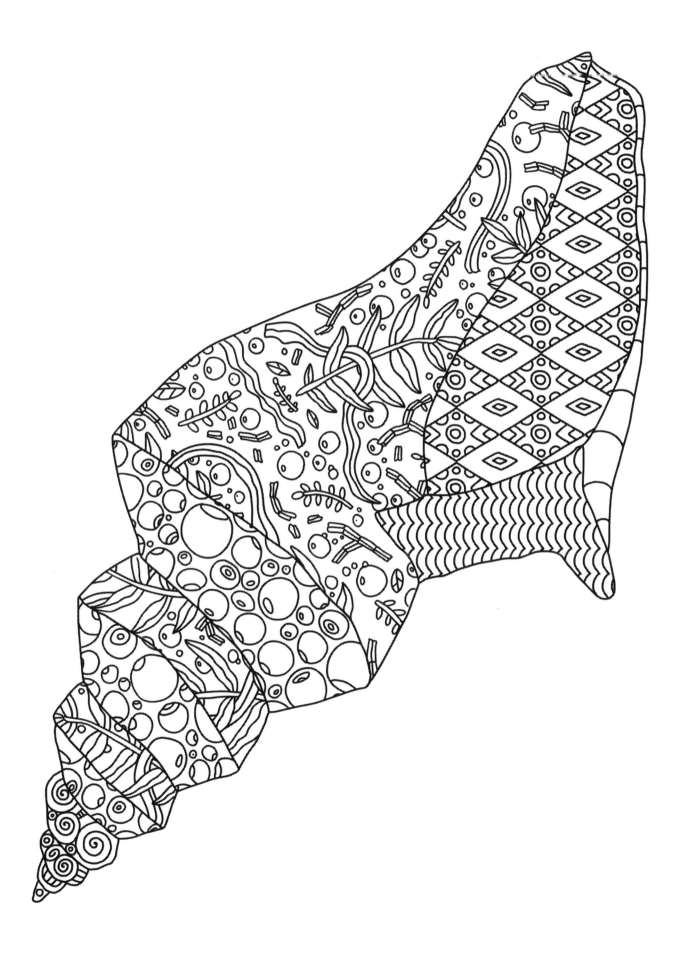

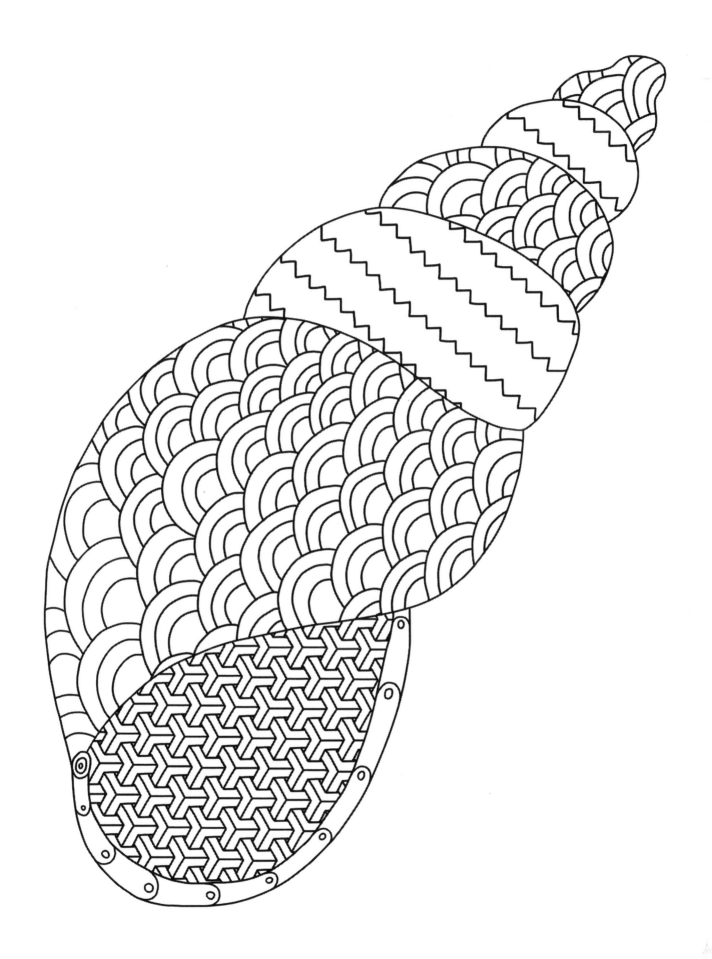

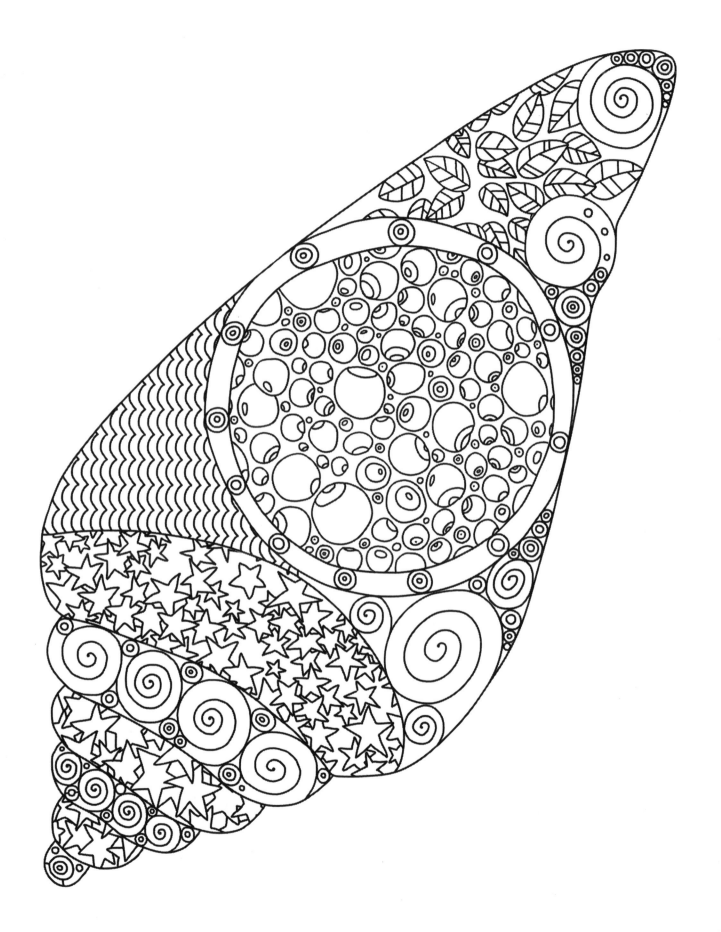

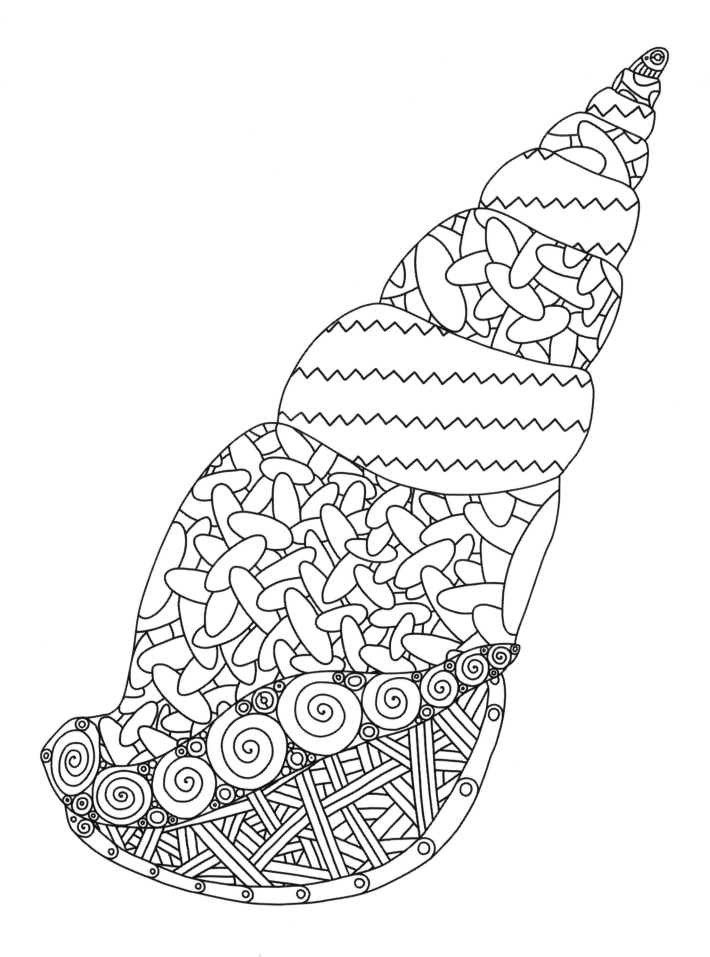

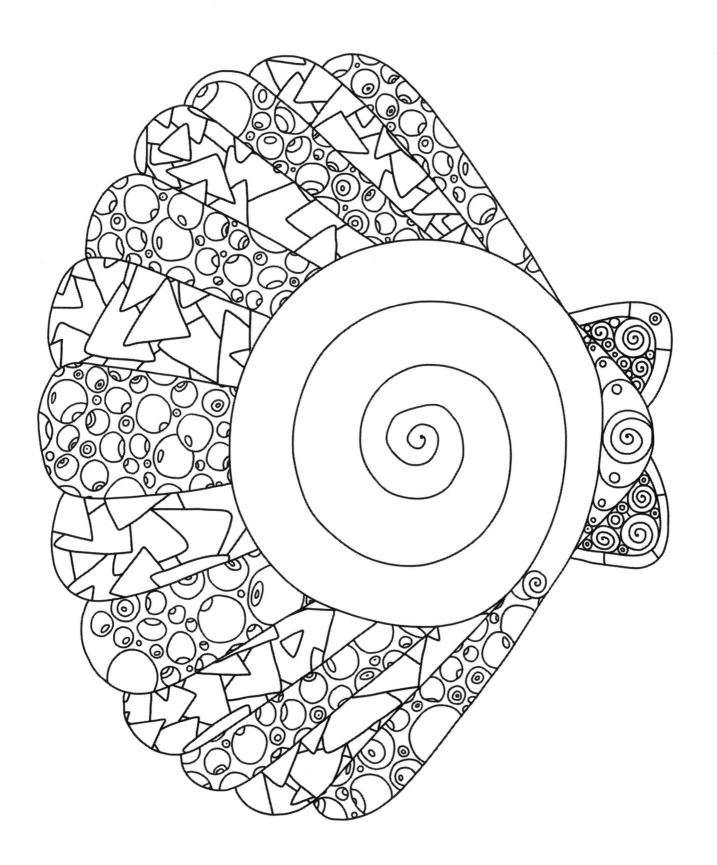

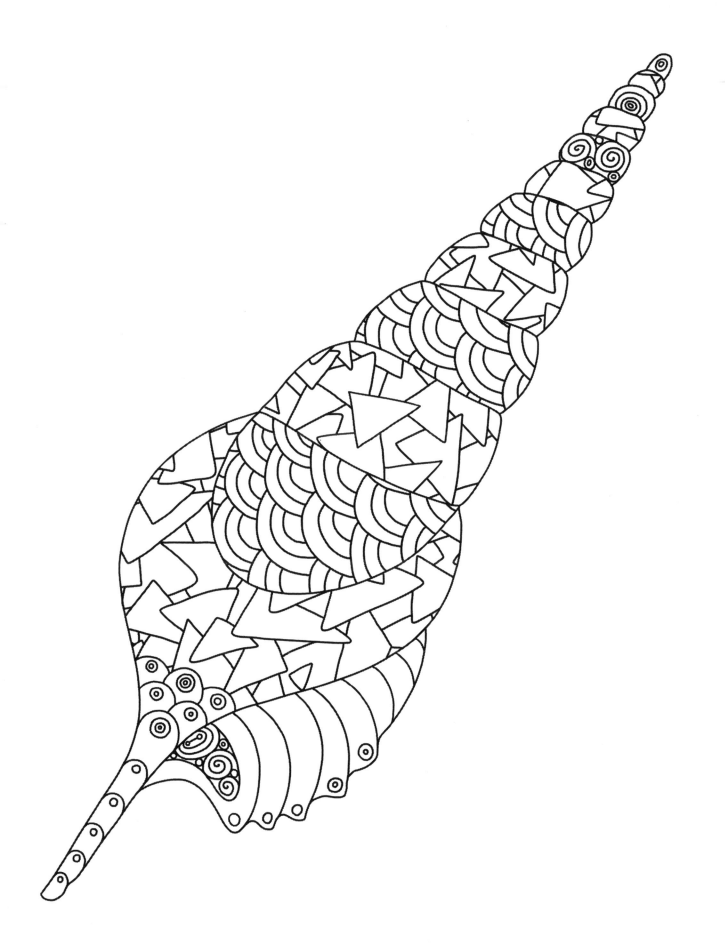

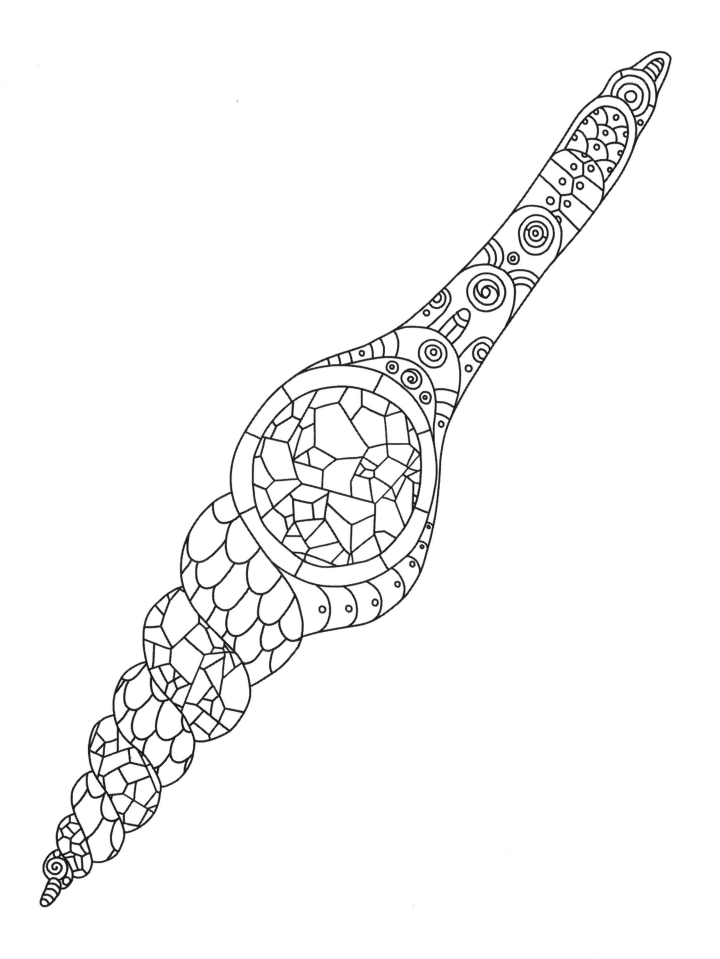

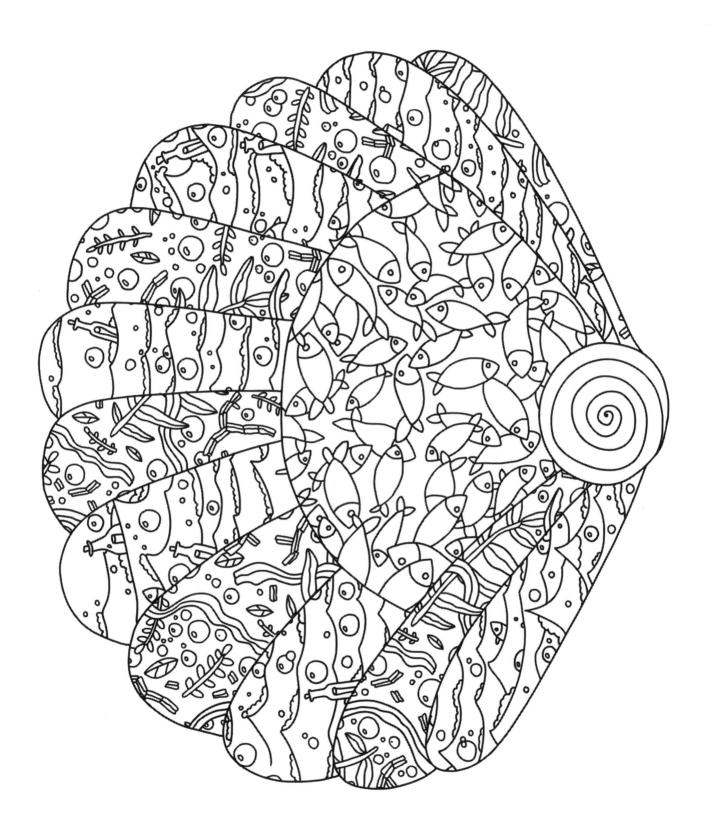

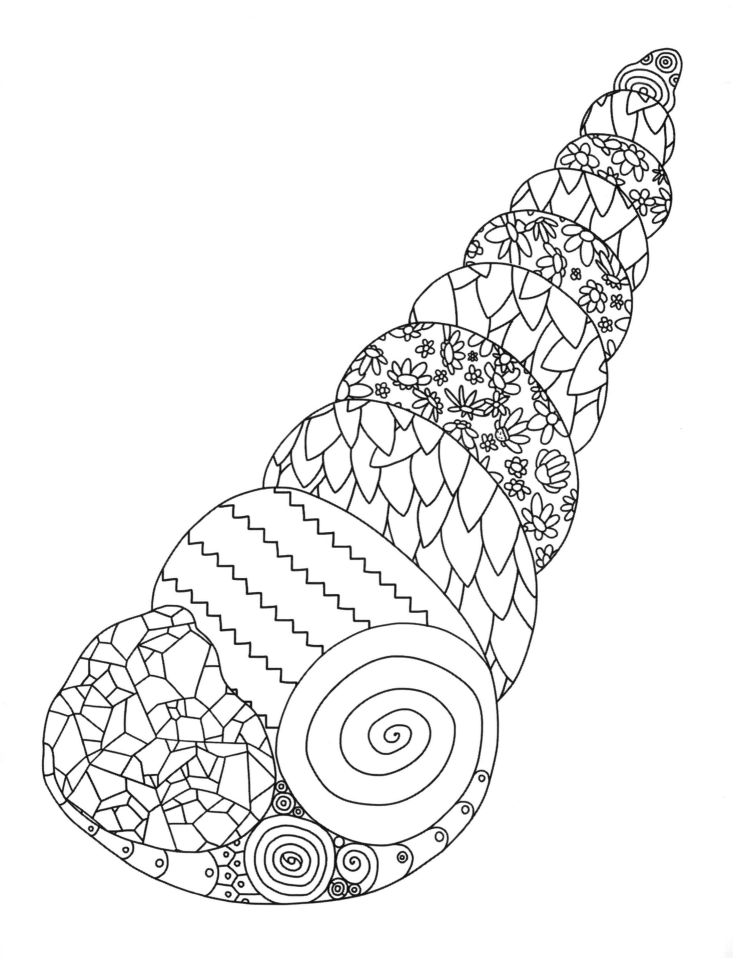

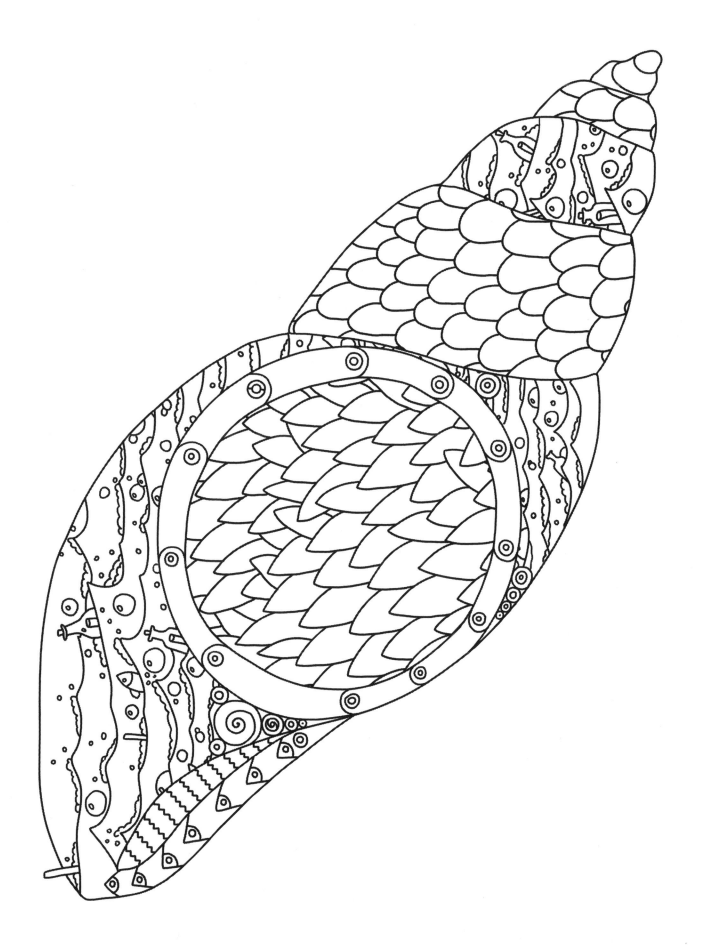

COLOR TEST PAGE

COLOR TEST PAGE